Preface

The study of Business Organization is fundamental to understanding how companies operate, grow, and sustain themselves in an ever-evolving market. As students, researchers, and professionals, mastering the principles and intricacies of business organization equips us with the knowledge and skills necessary to navigate the complexities of modern enterprises.

"IGNOU BCA Business Organisation Previous Year Unsolved Papers ECO 001" is designed to serve as a valuable resource for students preparing for exams, educators seeking supplementary material for instruction, and professionals aiming to refine their understanding of core business concepts. By presenting a comprehensive collection of unsolved questions from previous years' examinations, this book offers readers an opportunity to test their knowledge, enhance problem-solving skills, and gain deeper insights into the subject matter.

The questions included in this book have been meticulously curated from various academic and professional examinations. They cover a broad spectrum of topics within the domain of Business Organization, including but not limited to organizational structures, management principles, corporate governance, strategic planning, and the dynamics of business environments. The diversity of questions ensures that readers are exposed to various aspects of the subject, encouraging critical thinking and a holistic understanding.

One of the unique features of this book is its focus on unsolved questions. By engaging with these questions, readers are encouraged to actively apply their knowledge, develop independent thinking, and cultivate analytical abilities. This approach not only prepares students for examinations but also fosters a deeper appreciation for the complexities and challenges inherent in business organization.

In addition to serving as a study aid, this book can be a useful tool for educators in crafting assignments, class discussions, and practice tests. It allows instructors to gauge students' understanding and provides a basis for further exploration of the subject matter.

We would like to express our sincere gratitude to the students and educators who have contributed to the development of this book. Their insights and feedback have been invaluable in ensuring that this compilation meets the highest standards of academic excellence. As you embark on your journey through the world of business studies, we hope that this book will be a reliable companion in your academic and professional growth.

Index

Table of Contents

ECO-001

BACHELOR'S DEGREE PROGRAMME

Chapter 1: Term-End Examination, June- 2014

ELECTIVE COURSE : COMMERCE BUSINESS ORGANISATION

Time : **2** hours

Maximum Marks : **50** (Weigh tage 70%)

Note : Attempt both section - **A** and section - **B**.

SECTION-A

1. Attempt **any four** of the following : 20

(a) Distinguish between private limited company and public limited company.

(b) Write a short note on bank overdraft.

(c) How is Industrial Finance corporation of India helpful in the industrial development ?

(d) Explain the concept of speculation at stock exchanges.

(e) State with reasons of your choice of media of advertising for a low priced detergent in the rural areas.

(f) Describe briefly the importance of transport in trade.

(g) Enumerate the major reasons for the government participation in business.

(h) Distinguish between current bank account and savings bank accounts.

SECTION –B

Note : Attempt any three of the following :

2. What do you mean by partnership ? Enumerate the main features of partnership form of business organisation. 10

3. Define capital structure. Describe the factors that determine the capital structure of a company. 10

4. Discuss the primary and secondary functions of a stock exchange. 10

5. How does advertisement help the business ? Also state its adverse effects. 10

6. Outline the relationship between a banker and its customer. What are the obligations of a bank towards them ? 10

7. Describe the distinctive features of public utilities. 10

ECO-001

BACHELOR'S DEGREE PROGRAMME

Chapter 2: Term-End Examination, December- 2014

ELECTIVE COURSE : COMMERCE BUSINESS ORGANISATION

Time : **2** hours

Maximum Marks : **50** (Weightage 70%)

Note : Attempt both part- **A** and part - **B**.

PART-A

1. Distinguish between any two of the following : 10

(a) Wholesale trade and retail trade

(b) Entrepreneur and promoter

(c) Statutory company and registered company

(d) Publicity and advertisement

2. Write short notes on any two of the following : 10

(a) Bank overdraft

(b) Margin trading

(c) Outdoor media

(d) Bill of lading

PART-B

Attempt any three of the following questions :

3. What do you mean by business ? Describe salient features of business and discuss its economic objectives. 10

4. (a) Describe the functions of Industrial Development Bank of India (IDBI). 10

(b) How is it different from Industrial Finance Corporation of India OECD ?

5. What do you mean by foreign trade ? Discuss the importance of foreign trade. Explain the common problems faced in foreign trade. 10

6. What do you mean by risk management ? Explain the various steps followed in risk management. 10

7. "Efficient transportation is an integral part of economic growth". Elaborate. 10

8. What is meant by departmental form of organisation ? Discuss its merits and demerits. 10

ECO-001

BACHELOR'S DEGREE PROGRAMME

Chapter 3: Term-End Examination, June- 2015

ELECTIVE COURSE : COMMERCE BUSINESS ORGANISATION

Time : 2 hours

Maximum Marks : **50** (Weightage : 70%)

Note : Attempt both Part- **A** and Part - **B**.

PART A

1. Distinguish between any two of the following : 10

   (a) Fixed capital and working capital

   (b) Direct and indirect distribution channel

   (c) Departmental store and supermarket

   (d) Pledge and hypothecation

2. Write short notes on any two of the following : 10

   (a) Aids to trade

   (b) International financial institutions

   (c) Outdoor media

   (d) Insurable risk

PART – B

Attempt any three of the following questions :

3. What do you mean by a company ? Explain its salient features. 10

4. Outline the characteristics of stock exchange Describe its primary and secondary functions. 10

5. Define advertising and discuss types of media and their characteristics. 10

6. "Retailer is an important link in the supply chain of consumer goods." Elaborate by giving suitable examples. 10

7. What is meant by insurance ? Explain briefly various types of insurances. 10

8. What is meant by public utilities ? Describe the distinctive features of public utilities 10

ECO-001

BACHELOR'S DEGREE PROGRAMME

Chapter 4: Term-End Examination, December- 2015

ELECTIVE COURSE : COMMERCE BUSINESS ORGANISATION

Time : **2** hours

Maximum Marks : **50** (Weightage : 70%)

Note : Attempt both Part- **A** and Part - **B.**

PART A

1. Attempt any four of the following : 20

(a) Distinguish between non - economic and economic activities of human beings.

(b) State the qualities of a good entrepreneur.

(c) Describe the methods of raising long - term capital.

(d) State briefly the rules for listing of securities on a stock exchange.

(e) Distinguish between advertisement and publicity.

(f) State channels of distribution of industrial goods

PART - B

Attempt any three of the following questions :

2. What is meant by cooperative form of organisation ? Enumerate its main features. 10

3. What is meant by long - term finance ? Describe various sources of long - term finance. 10

4. How does speculation differ from gambling ? State the various factors affecting prices of securities in a stock exchange. 10

5. Explain the difference between functional and merchant middlemen. How do they help the business activities ? 10

6. How do commercial banks contribute to the economic development of a country ? Explain. 10

7. State the merits and demerits of government participation in business. 10

ECO-001

BACHELOR'S DEGREE PROGRAMME

Chapter 5: Term-End Examination, June 2016

ELECTIVE COURSE : COMMERCE BUSINESS ORGANISATION

Time : **2** hours

Maximum Marks : **50** (Weightage : 70%)

Note : Attempt both Part - **A** and Part - **B**.

PART – A

1. Attempt any four of the following : 20

(a) Distinguish between entrepreneur and promoter.

(b) State the characteristics of a capital market.

(c) Explain forward delivery contracts at the stock exchange.

(d) State the various outdoor media of advertising.

(e) Enumerate essentials of a good transport system.

(f) How does a public enterprise differ from private enterprise ? Explain.

PART – B

Attempt any three of the following :

2. Name the four forms of business organisation. Describe briefly the requisites of an ideal form of business organisation. 10

3. What is a stock exchange ? Describe briefly its various functions. 10

4. Suppose your company has launched a detergent of low price. As the chief of the marketing wing, how will you choose an appropriate media for making it popular ? 10

5. State the importance of distribution channel in the promotion of business. Describe briefly the factors that influence the choice of the channel. 10

6. Suppose your company decides to set up a manufacturing unit of apparels. How will you proceed for importing the necessary machinery and technology for the same ? Explain. 10

7. What do you mean by risk management ? Describe briefly the insurable risks and the non - insurable risks. 10

ECO-001

BACHELOR'S DEGREE PROGRAMME

Chapter 6: Term-End Examination, December- 2016

ELECTIVE COURSE : COMMERCE BUSINESS ORGANISATION

Time : **2** Hours

Maximum Marks : **50** (Weightage : 70%)

Note : Attempt any five questions. All questions carry equal marks.

1. Define the term 'business' and state its essential features. How is it different from profession ? 10

2. What do you mean by cooperative form of organization ? Explain its merits and limitations. 10

3. What are the various methods of raising short-term capital ? Explain them briefly. 10

4. Discuss the various functions performed by wholesalers. 10

5. Distinguish between any two of the following : 10

(a) Loan and Overdraft

(b) Cash Credit and Overdraft

(c) Pledge and Hypothecation

6. Explain the features of a fire policy and state the various types of fire policies issued by insurance companies. 10

7. What is a public enterprise ? State the features and objectives of a public enterprise. 10

8. Write short notes on any two of the following : 10

(a) Departmental Store

(b) Public Corporation

(c) Pricing policy followed by public utilities

ECO-001

BACHELOR'S DEGREE PROGRAMME

Chapter 6: Term-End Examination, December- 2017

ELECTIVE COURSE : COMMERCE BUSINESS ORGANISATION

Time : **2** Hours

Maximum Marks : **50** (Weightage : 70%)

Note : Attempt both Part -**A** and Part - **B.**

PART – A

1. Attempt any four of the following : 20

(a) Briefly explain the advantages of raising funds through the issue of debentures.

(b) Differentiate between business and profession.

(c) Explain the concept of 'entrepreneurship'.

(d) Write a short note on 'Recurring Deposit Account'.

(e) What are the essentials of a good transport system ?

(f) State the objectives of Public Enterprises.

PART – B

Attempt any three of the following questions :

2. What do you mean by 'business risk' ? Explain the process of risk management. 10

3. What is meant by Public Utility Undertaking ? Discuss the broad aspects of their pricing policies. 10

4. What is a stock exchange ? Explain the factors affecting the prices at a stock exchange. 10

5. Briefly describe the role of an entrepreneur in business promotion. How does an entrepreneur differ from a promoter ? 10

6. Explain the significance of foreign trade for a country, and state the problems encountered in foreign trade by Indian entrepreneurs. 10

ECO-001

BACHELOR'S DEGREE PROGRAMME

Chapter 7: Term-End Examination, June- 2018

ELECTIVE COURSE : COMMERCE BUSINESS ORGANISATION

Time : **2** Hours

Maximum Marks : **50** (Weightage : 70%)

Note : Attempt both Part - **A** and Part - **B.**

PART – A

1. Attempt any four of the following : 20

(a) Write a short note on 'underwriting'.

(b) Differentiate between Advertisement and Publicity.

(c) State the services rendered by the retailers to the consumers.

(d) Briefly explain the merits of Partnership form of organisation.

(e) Briefly explain the procedure of raising funds through public deposits.

(f) State the problems of Public Enterprises.

PART – B

Attempt any three of the following questions :

2. Define 'Advertising Media'. State its different types and the requisites of an ideal medium. 10

3. What are the various modes of creating charge ? Explain them briefly. 10

4. What is a 'Public Corporation? Explain its merits and limitations. 10

5. What is a joint stock company ? Explain its limitations as a form of business organisation. 10

6. Write short notes on any two of the following : 10

(a) Aids to trade

(b) Money market

(c) Channel of distribution

(d) Procedure of Import trade

ECO-001

BACHELOR'S DEGREE PROGRAMME

Chapter 8: Term-End Examination, December- 2018

ELECTIVE COURSE : COMMERCE BUSINESS ORGANISATION

Time : **2** hours

Maximum Marks **50** (Weightage : 70%)

Note : Attempt both Part - **A** and Part - **B.**

PART – A

1. Attempt any four of the following : 20

(a) Enumerate the essentials of an effective advertisement.

(b) Briefly explain the services provided by retailers to consumers.

(c) List out the factors affecting the capital structure of a firm.

(d) Distinguish between 'Entrepreneur' and 'Promoter'.

(e) Explain the benefits of containerisation for transportation of goods.

(f) State the features of public utilities.

PART – B

Attempt any three questions :

2. Explain the financial performance of public enterprises in India. 10

3. "All business risks are not insurable". In the light of this statement, explain insurable risks and non-insurable risks. 10

4. Define the term 'business' and explain its essential features. 10

5. Describe 'factoring' and 'discounting of bills of exchange' as methods of raising short-term finance. 10

6. Explain the objectives of advertising. 10

7. (a)Discuss how does a letter of credit help in financing foreign trade. 10

(b) Narrate the shipping documents required to be submitted along with a documentary letter of credit.

ECO-001

BACHELOR'S DEGREE PROGRAMME

Chapter 9: Term-End Examination, June- 2019

ELECTIVE COURSE : COMMERCE BUSINESS ORGANISATION

Time : **2** Hours

Maximum Marks : **50** (Weightage : 70%)

Note : Attempt any five questions. All questions carry equal marks.

1. Distinguish between the following : 10

   (a) Ownership capital and Borrowed capital.

   (b) Business and Commerce

2. Explain the concept of 'Business' and describe the objectives of business. 10

3. What is cooperative form of business organisation ? Explain the features of a cooperative form of organisation. 10

4. What are the various types of business risks ? Discuss the various steps involved in risk management. 10

5. What is a public utility ? Explain its features. 10

6. Outline the factors which influence the choice of distribution channel. 10

7. Discuss various methods of raising short-term capital. 10

8. Explain the relationship between a banker and its customer. 10

ECO-001

BACHELOR'S DEGREE PROGRAMME

Chapter 10: Term-End Examination, December- 2019

ELECTIVE COURSE : COMMERCE BUSINESS ORGANISATION

Time : **2** Hours

Maximum : Marks : **50** (Weightage : 70%)

Note: Attempt both Part-**A** and **B.**

Part-A

Attempt any four of the following: 20

Differentiate between:

(a) Business and commerce

(b) Capital market and money market

(c) Intensive distribution and exclusive distribution

(d) Government Enterprise and Public Limited Company

(e) Super market and Departmental store

(f) Equity shares and preference shares.

Part-B

2. Mention various prerequisites for deciding an ideal form of Business Organisation? 10

3. What is 'Capital Structure'? What are the various factors determining the capital structure? 10

4. Write short notes on any two of the following: 10

(a) Distinction between Entrepreneur and Intrapreneur

(b) Factoring

(c) Foreign sources for raising capital

(d) Arguments against advertising

5. What do you understand by 'Bank'? Explain various types of banks. 10

6. Explain sea transportation Tabulate its classification based on area of operation? Mention its procedure? 10

ECO-001

BACHELOR'S DEGREE PROGRAMME

Chapter 11: Term-End Examination, December- 2020

BUSINESS ORGANIZATION

Time : **2** Hours Maximum Marks : **50**

Note : Attempt both the Parts **'A'** and **'B'** as directed.

Part—A

1. Distinguish between any two of the following : 10

(a) Business and profession

(b) Equity shares and debentures

(c) Functional middlemen and merchant middlemen

(d) Life insurance and other forms of insurance

2. Write short notes on any two of the following : 10

(a) Monopolistic position of public utilities

(b) Pervasiveness of risks in business

(c) Requisites of an ideal medium of advertising

(d) Retained profits as a source of long-term finance

Part—B

Note : Attempt any three of the following questions.

3. "Company form of business organisation is the most ideal form of business organisation suitable for all types of business." Discuss. 10

4. Explain the factors be kept in mind while determining the capital structure of a company. 10

5. "Advertising is a social waste." Do you agree with this statement ? Give reasons for your argument. 10

6. Discuss various modes of creating charge by banks on the tangible assets of the borrowers. 10

7. Why is it necessary for the Government to directly participate in business ? Discuss. 10

ECO-001

BACHELOR'S DEGREE PROGRAMME

Chapter 12: Term-End Examination, June- 2021

ELECTIVE COURSE : COMMERCE BUSINESS ORGANISATION

Time : **2** hours

Maximum Marks : **50** (Weightage : 70%)

Note : Attempt both Part **A** and Part **B.**

PART A

1. Distinguish between any two of the following : 10

(a) Commerce and Trade

(b) Fixed capital and Working capital

(c) Bill of Lading and Shipping Bill

(d) Public Enterprise and Public Limited Company

2. Write short notes on any two of the following : 10

(a) Relationship between banker and customer

(b) Direct channels of distribution

(c) Listing of securities on a stock exchange

(d) Characteristics of an entrepreneur

Part B

Attempt any **three** of the following questions :

3. ''Partnership form of business organisation overcomes the limitations of sole proprietorship form of organisation.'' Discuss. 10

4. What are the main features of a Government Company ? How is a Government Company different from a statutory corporation ? 10

5. Briefly discuss various sources of long term finance of the company. 10

6. Discuss various problems of foreign trade in the Indian context. 10

7. ''All types of business risks are insurable.'' Comment. 10

ECO-001

BACHELOR'S DEGREE PROGRAMME

Chapter 13: Term-End Examination, December- 2021

ELECTIVE COURSE : COMMERCE BUSINESS ORGANISATION

Time : **2** hours

Maximum Marks : **50** (Weightage : 70%)

Note : Attempt both Part **A** and Part **B.**

PART A

1. Differentiate between any two of the following : 10

(a) Profession and Employment

(b) Bonded warehouse and Public warehouse

(c) Publicity and Advertisement

2. Write short notes on any two of the following : 10

(a) Internal Trade and External Trade

(b) Partnership Deed

(c) Methods of Raising Capital

(d) Factors Affecting Choice of Media

PART B

Attempt any **three** of the following questions :

3. Explain the term Entrepreneurship. What are the characteristics of an entrepreneur ? Mention their functions. 10

4. Explain the role of different 'special financial institutions' for raising long-term finance for business. 10

5. What do you understand by the term 'Foreign Trade' ? Briefly explain the export-import procedure. 10

6. Elaborate the term 'Business Risks'. Explain the importance of Insurance in overcoming these risks. 10

7. What is 'Containerisation' ? How is it different from warehousing ? Explain. 10

ECO-001

BACHELOR'S DEGREE PROGRAMME

(BDP)

Chapter 14: Term-End Examination, June, 2022

ELECTIVE COURSE : COMMERCE BUSINESS ORGANISATION

Time : **2** Hours

Maximum Marks : **50** Weightage : 70%

Note : (i) Attempt any five questions. (ii) All questions carry equal marks.

1. Describe the requisites of an ideal form of business organisation. 10

2. Discuss main features of sole trader organisation. State briefly its merits and limitations. 10

3. Differentiate between advertisement and publicity with suitable example. 10

4. Discuss briefly the factors that influence the choice of channel of distribution. 10

5. What are the various types of risks that are associated with any business ? Discuss briefly. 10

6. In what respect is rail transport superior to road transport ? What are the limitations of rail transport ? 10

7. What is a public enterprise ? How is it different from private enterprise ? 10

8. Write short notes on any two of the following : 10

(a) Departmental organisation

(b) Sales policy of public utilities service institutions.

(c) Instruments of government control of private business

(d) Government company

ECO-001

BACHELOR'S DEGREE PROGRAMME

Chapter 15: Term-End Examination, December- 2022

ELECTIVE COURSE : COMMERCE BUSINESS ORGANISATION

Time : **2** hours

Maximum Marks : **50** (Weightage : 70%)

Note : Attempt any five questions . All questions carry equal marks.

1. What is a Government Company ? How is it different from a Non-Government Company ? 10

2. Examine the problems that are involved in Foreign trade. 10

3. What are the services that are provided by retailers in a business ? Discuss with example. 10

4. Describe the role of commercial banks in the economic development of a country. 10

5. "Risk is pervasive in business." Elaborate with example. 10

6. Discuss briefly insurable risks and non-insurable risks with suitable example. 10

7. Differentiate between life insurance and other forms of insurance. 10

8. Write short notes on any two of the following : 10

(a) Promoter vs. Entrepreneur

(b) Public Limited Company

(c) Joint Hindu Family Firm

(d) Partnership Form of Organisation

ECO-001

BACHELOR'S DEGREE PROGRAMME

(BDP)

Chapter 16: Term-End Examination, June- 2023

ELECTIVE COURSE : COMMERCE BUSINESS ORGANISATION

Time : **2** Hours

Maximum Marks : **50**

Note : Attempt any five question. All questions carry equal marks.

1. What do you understand by Business Organization ? What are the basic forms of Business Organisation ? 10

2. What do you understand by Sole Trader Organisation ? State the merits and limitations of Sole Trader Organisation. 10

3. Compare the relative advantages and disadvantages of issuing equity shares and preference shares. 10

4. "Foreign trade is an engine of economic growth in a country." Discuss this statement. 10

5. What is Bank ? Discuss the types of accounts in a Bank. 10

6. What is Public Utility Undertaking ? State its essential characteristics. 10

7. Discuss instruments of government control on private business. 10

8. Write short notes on any two of the following : 10

(a) Types of Business Risk

(b) Classification of Commerce

(c) Kinds of Insurance

(d) Letter of Credit

ECO–01

BACHELOR'S DEGREE PROGRAMME

(BDP)

Chapter 17: Term-End Examination, December, 2023

ELECTIVE COURSE : COMMERCE BUSINESS ORGANISATION

Time : **2** Hours

Maximum Marks : **50** Weightage : 70%

Note : Attempt any five questions. All questions carry equal marks.

1. What is Business ? Explain features and objectives of Business. 10

2. What is Industry ? Explain its classification with illustrations. 10

3. Differentiate between Partnership and Joint Stock Company. 10

4. Briefly explain the meaning of the following : 10

(a) Money Market

(b) Capital Market

(c) New Issue Market

5. What is Media ? Discuss the characteristics and types of media. 10

6. Outline the nature of problems and limitations associated with the operation of public enterprises. 10

7. What is channel of distribution system ? Discuss the factors influencing the choice of channel. 10

8. Write short notes on any two of the following : 10

(a) Economic Activity vs. Non-Economic Activity

(b) Wholesalers vs. Retailers

(c) Ownership Capital vs. Borrowed Capital

(d) Various types of Banks

Printed at Repro India Ltd.